CW00349474

MINI
MATT
Family Matters

The Daily Telegraph

'We've just voted you
out of the house'

Family Matters

ORION

Orion Books
A division of the Orion Publishing Group Ltd
Orion House
5 Upper St Martin's Lane
London
WC2H 9EA

This collected edition first published by
Orion Books Ltd in 2004

A CIP catalogue record for this book
is available from the British Library

ISBN 0 75285 971 4

Printed and bound in Great Britain by
Clays Ltd, St Ives plc

www.orionbooks.co.uk

FOREWORD

Matt's world is immediately recognisable and all his characters familiar. You always know where you are, and who you are with, in his cartoons. He is a master of the essential, perfect detail; the flowery curtains, the garden fence, the porter's trolley, the tweedy jacket, the unshaven chin, the drystone wall – the list is endless – set the scene with apparently effortless precision.

His characters are sometimes enraged, on rare occasions triumphant, now and then temporarily defeated. But most often they are perplexed, and confront life with a kind of hopeful desperation. And somehow, as you laugh at their comical plight, you feel oddly reassured that you too will make it through.

Nicholas Garland

MINI
MATT
Family Matters

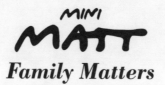

'My accountant says we
should get drunk and
start a family'

'If anyone here knows of
any reason why these two
people cannot move their
stuff into a flat . . .'

'And can you keep my
daughter in the tent to which she
has become accustomed?'

'How much does Sir want to spend?
They range from prudent to
gigantic economic miscalculation'

'Before you say no, let me outline
some of the tax benefits . . .'

'Are you friends of the bride or of the groom's first wife?'

'By the way, I might have some
problems with those vows'

'We don't consider two Tories
to be a calm and stable
environment for a child'

'He's feeding well but I'm
worried that he still hasn't
done anything about
his pension'

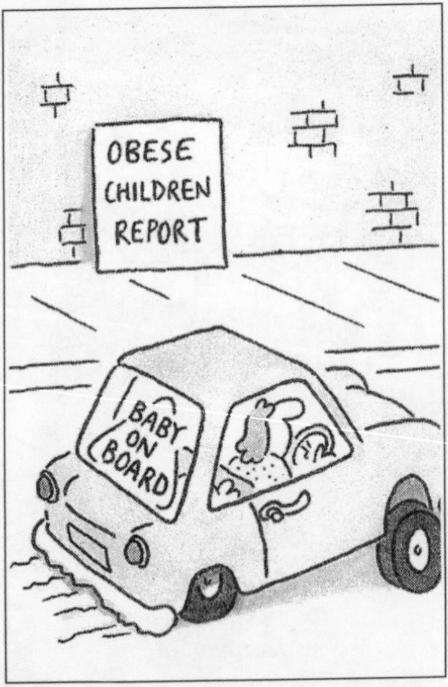
OBESE
CHILDREN
REPORT
BABY ON BOARD

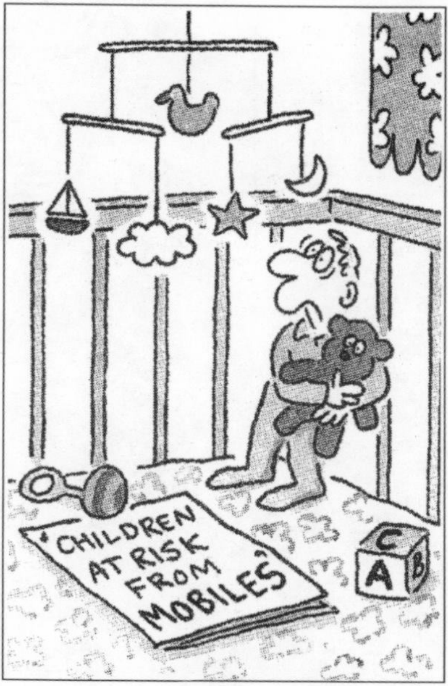

'CHILDREN AT RISK FROM MOBILES'
C
A
B

'When I was your age we had to make our own accidents'

'And here's a lollipop
for being so brave'

'One day, son, when
you're older, I'd like you
to explain all this to me'

'Phew, if my sister
hadn't told me about
Mad Chocolate, I might
have eaten that Easter egg'

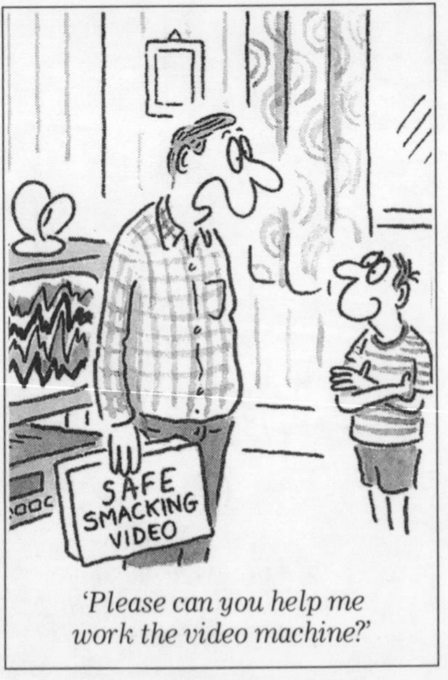
SAFE
SMACKING
VIDEO

'Please can you help me work the video machine?'

'We have reason to believe you
have a child that hasn't been
taken to the Harry Potter film'

'This hurts me more
than it hurts you, Dad'

'I've hidden the
TV remote control'

'I'm attempting to combine
the two roles of not working
and not being a royal'

'It's a rat race, you take
the test at seven, and you're
burned out by eight'

'Go to bed or the Harry
Potter book gets it'

'Dad, I advise you
to do a runner'

'Scientists have discovered
a link between not eating
your greens and being hit
with a saucepan'

'Can Jimmy come out
to play football?'

'There's so much pressure,
having to juggle motherhood
with double geography'

'Apparently, selection
will be based on a
penalty shoot-out'

'Dad, believe me, £5,000 to miss
double maths is a bargain'

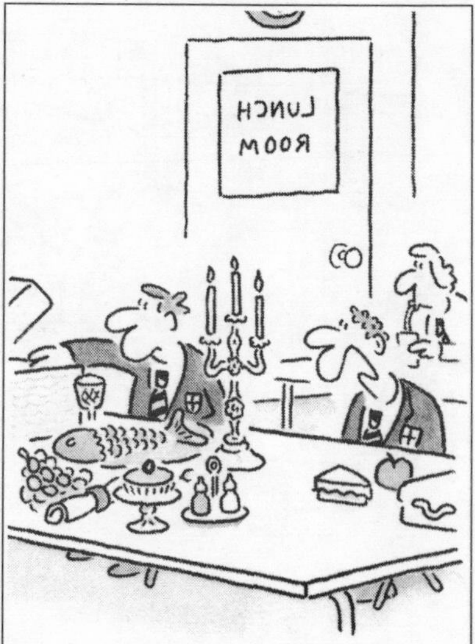
LUNCH
ROOM

'I wish I had gay parents'

'At least we know you're
not taking performance-
enhancing drugs'

'It's much harder to fail
exams than it was in your day'

'Shall we wake him and
tell him to stop worrying?'

'Would you get the report
on nepotism from my
mummy's office, please'

'I put the clocks forward –
was there something else I
was supposed to remember?'

'Too old to be a teenage mum, too young for menopause reversal'

'Dad, just because you give
me pocket money, don't
expect any special favours'

'Dad, can I borrow the go-kart?'

'I'm going to get my
husband to do mine'

'We call him The Dome;
he's very expensive and
we can't get rid of him'

'Your university days are some
of the happiest of my life'

'GAY? I suppose that
means I'll have to pay
for your wedding!'

'If your mother comes for Christmas, I want her to swear an oath that she'll fit in with our way of life'

'I've either just done our
weekly shop at Tesco,
or I've adopted twins'

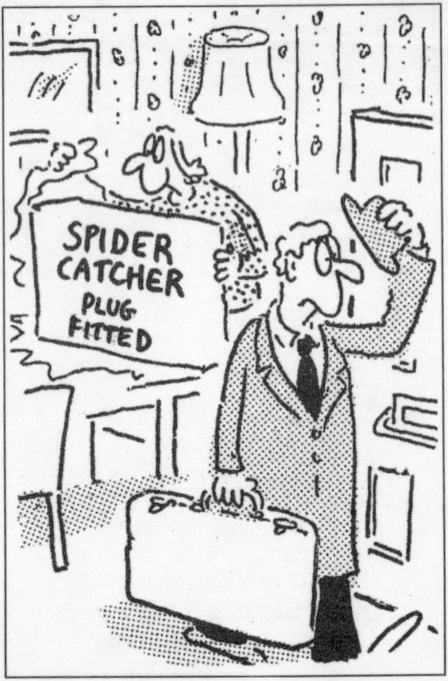
SPIDER
CATCHER
PLUG
FITTED

'If your mother comes here
for Christmas I will exercise
my right to demonstrate'

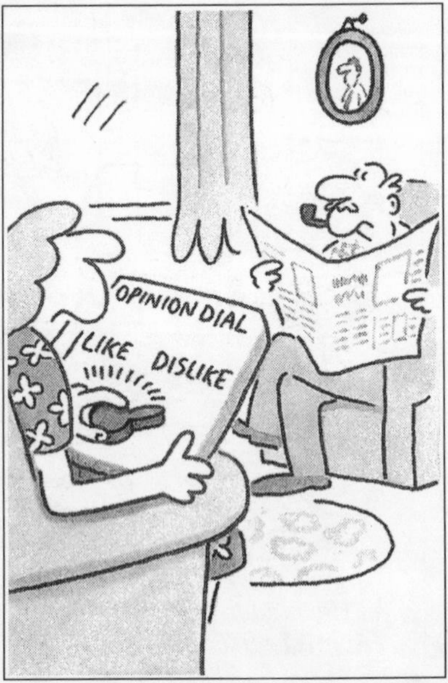
OPINION DIAL
LIKE
DISLIKE

'He tried to switch off the
final episode of Morse'

'I suppose that's another
one of those jobs you'll
never get round to doing'

'Darling please don't leave
me – I'll have to fill in the
census form all over again'

'I was married during Back to
Basics and divorced just as
Supporting Families
was launched'

'I suppose this is
goodbye, then'

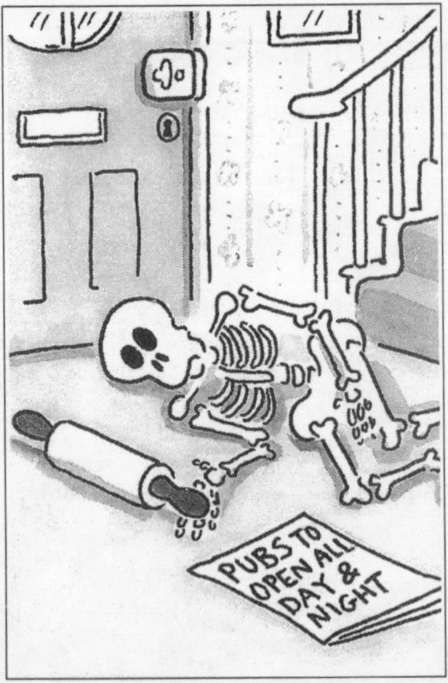
PUBS TO OPEN ALL DAY & NIGHT

'I was abandoned as a
baby and brought up by
by-pass protesters'

'Nobody understands me . . . shut
up. . . I hate you . . . I'm going out'